Tatanka-Iyotanka

A Biography of

SITTING BULL

by Michael Crummett

WESTERN NATIONAL PARKS ASSOCIATION
TUCSON, ARIZONA

contents

"I WOULD RATHER DIE AN INDIAN THAN LIVE A WHITE MAN!"

Sitting Bull, 1888

In the tipi rings of Northern Plains tribes, he was the bravest of warriors; his sixty-three conspicuous coups left him with few peers. His prowess with bow and arrow was surpassed only by his generosity in sharing with the less fortunate. And he was a powerful medicine man and inspired prophet who lived Indian religion in his daily life and renewed it annually in the grueling Lakota Sun Dance.

Sitting Bull was revered by his own people as a wise, compassionate leader and a daring fighter. Though he was moderately short in stature, his presence loomed large on the northern Plains. For thirty years he carefully piloted his people through their ever-shrinking natural and political domain while resisting the incursions of the European-American. Sitting Bull dedicated himself to the traditional culture of the Lakota and fought hard to preserve it.

Sitting Bull's name was indelibly etched on the pages of American history when the Lakota and Cheyenne overwhelmingly defeated an attack by the U.S. Army's Seventh Cavalry under Lt. Col. George Armstrong Custer at the Battle of the Little Bighorn.

Wooden Leg, a Northern Cheyenne who fought at Little Bighorn, described Sitting Bull's power and popularity at the time of the battle: "He had come now into admiration by all Indians as a man whose medicine was good—that is, as a man having a kind heart and good judgment as to the best course of conduct. He was considered as being altogether brave, but peaceable. No man in the Lakota

Nation was braver in battle than Sitting Bull. He asked none of his warriors to take any chances that he was not willing at all times to share. He was strong in the Indian religion. He made medicine many times."

Today, Sitting Bull is embraced with respect and pride by Indians because of the vigilance with which he led the Lakota people through the harsh times of the late 1800s. Contemporary Hunkpapa are especially honored to have one of their own holy men as the last to leave the open prairie for the reservation.

Isaac Dog Eagle, a Hunkpapa of sixty years and fifth-generation descendant of Sitting Bull, is convinced that modern-day Lakota "see the great things that Sitting Bull did for his people. And a lot of our men know what Sitting Bull stood for." Continuing, he boasts, "You can see young kids today go around talking about 'here's where grandpa Sitting Bull used to be' or 'here's where grandpa Sitting Bull did this thing or that thing.' That is good! We need that."

⤨

TATANKA-IYOTANKA

MEANS *SITTING BULL* IN THE

LANGUAGE OF THE HUNKPAPA.

*M*any people call the northern plains home. Some are related by blood or by language; others are not. The chart on the facing page shows the relationship between the Lakota, Nakota, and Dakota people. Tatanka-Iyotanka (Sitting Bull) was born into the Hunkpapa clan and was one of the respected leaders of all the Lakota clans.

European settlers and soldiers often used the Chippewa term "Sioux" for all the Dakota people. In this book, we use the name of the specific clan or the terms "Lakota" and "Teton."

Other people living on the northern plains but not related to the Dakota group are the Arikara, Assiniboine, Northern Cheyenne, Cree, Crow, Flathead, Gros Ventre, Hidatsa, and Mandan.

TRIBAL TREE

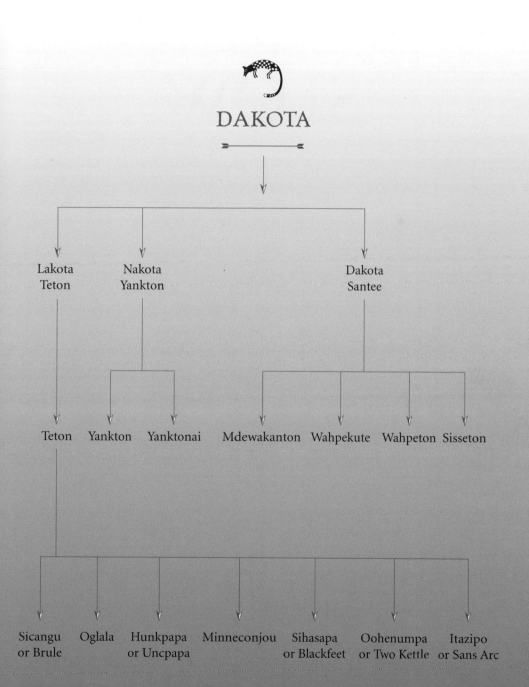

A Boy Named SLOW

Sitting Bull's life began on the Ree (Grand) River around March of 1831. His parents, Jumping Bull and Her-Holy-Door, named him "Slow" because he was gentle, deliberate, and slightly bowlegged. He slew his first buffalo when he was ten and gave the meat away to some tribal elders who could not hunt and had little food. Eventually, Slow excelled at foot races and, ironically, became the fastest runner in the Hunkpapa tribe.

He received a new name when he struck his first coup in the Powder River Valley. Ten men and an unproven boy set out for Crow country looking for horses and possible coups (that is, being the first to strike an enemy with a coup stick or other weapon). Slow's body was painted yellow from head to toe as he sat astride his father's large gray horse.

In the distance, the Hunkpapa warriors saw a dozen Crow pausing by a stream. Slow broke into the lead, urging his fast steed to a full gallop and yelling out a war cry as he charged the startled foes. The Crow mounted their horses and scattered. The reckless Slow picked one out, quickly overtook and struck him with his coup stick, and sent the Crow man tumbling to the ground. Another Hunkpapa rushed in to count second coup and finish him off.

When the war party returned to the Powder River encampment, Slow's father followed tradition in announcing his son's first coup at fourteen. For such a spectacular display of courage, his father paid the ultimate compliment of love and pride by giving him his own name, *Tatanka-Iyotanka,* or "Sitting Bull." His name described the huge male buffalo who was tough in conflict and afraid of nothing. Sometimes it would sit down on its rump to fight on to the death. His father took the name "Jumping Bull" from then on.

To recognize Sitting Bull's valor at such a young age, Jumping Bull placed a single eagle feather upright in his son's hair, painted his entire body black to signify victory, put him on one of his favorite bay horses, and paraded him around the camps so that the Hunkpapas could cheer their new warrior. Sitting Bull proudly carried a circular buffalo shield given to him by his father. It was inscribed with sacred designs, imbued with spiritual power, and decorated with four eagle feathers hanging from the bottom of the shield's frame.

From this first coup, Sitting Bull went on to other exploits of courage and skill. One autumn, the Hunkpapa needed horses and decided to relieve the Crow of some of theirs. A hundred warriors moved along the Yellowstone River until they were near a Crow camp. Waiting until night, several warriors quietly sneaked into the camp and made off with a huge herd.

By daybreak, a large group of Crow was in hot pursuit. Several Hunkpapa, including Sitting Bull, dismounted to meet the irate

GRAND RIVER

followers. One of the Crow jumped off his horse, proudly wearing his red, ermine-trimmed, chief shirt. When the chief and Sitting Bull were in range, they aimed their guns. The Crow fired first, his flintlock ball tearing into the sole of Sitting Bull's left foot. Then Tatanka-Iyotanka shot and, after the smoke cleared, the Crow leader lay mortally wounded. Limping to his adversary, Sitting Bull drew his knife and thrust it into the enemy's heart. When the other Crow saw what had happened to their chief, they retreated.

Sitting Bull was not always a fierce combatant ready to inflict the worst. Sometimes, he would surprise his people by doing the exact opposite. On one occasion they went north to raid the Hohe (Assiniboine). The Hunkpapa warriors rode their horses through the unseasonable cold to where the Yellowstone flows into the Missouri River, not far from where soldiers would later build Fort Union and Fort Buford. In an open field of snow, they saw a solitary tipi lodging one Hohe family. When some of the Hunkpapa arrived, a mother with an infant and young son tried running away while the father fought to cover their flight. But with many attacking few, the Hohe attempts were in vain and soon four lay dead in the snow. One eleven-year-old boy remained.

The young Hohe stood with one arrow left in his bow, surrounded by those who had just killed his family. Three Hunkpapas took turns counting coups on him. Just as it looked as though his fate was sealed, Sitting Bull rode up to join the fray. Seeing something warm and reasonable in Tatanka-Iyotanka's face, the Hohe cried, "Big Brother, Big Brother, have pity on me."

With compassion for the frail but valiant Hohe, Sitting Bull jumped off his pony, ran to the lad's side, and embraced him. "Don't shoot," Sitting Bull exclaimed. "This boy is too brave to die. I have no brother. I take this one for my brother." When they returned to camp, an adoption ceremony took place. Sitting Bull gave away some horses and held a feast in his new brother's honor. The captive boy was called "Little Assiniboine" and developed into a fearless, well-liked man who chose never to return to the Hohe. After Sitting Bull's father died, he was given the name "Jumping Bull" and eventually became chief of the Strong Hearts, a distinguished society of Lakota warriors. He was loyal to Sitting Bull to the end.

Growing to LEADERSHIP

Each Lakota tribe usually had its own chief, council of elders (advisers), executive officers ("shirt wearers"), and warrior societies ("Strong Hearts" and "Silent Eaters"). Having proven himself on the battlefield, Sitting Bull was inducted into the Strong Hearts, the Hunkpapa warrior society. He quickly became one of two sash-wearers of the Strong Hearts (the brave sashwearer would stake his own ankle to the ground, remain there throughout combat, and leave only when one of his fellow fighters freed him after the battle). Soon, Sitting Bull founded the elite "Midnight Strong Hearts" warrior band and in no time was elevated to their distinguished leader. In 1857, at 26, he was promoted to tribal war chief.

Four Lakota chiefs—Running Antelope, Red Horn, Loud Voiced Hawk, and Four Horns—had directed tribal affairs since 1851 but were no longer fulfilling the expectations and goals of the tribal membership. Tough weather, frequent battles, and inadequate buffalo hunts led the tribe to question their chiefs' ability. Having fallen from grace and popularity, the four chiefs were subjected to secret testing to determine if each had the dignity, forbearance, generosity, wisdom, and great heart required for the high office of chief. Only Four Horns passed the test.

10

The shame and dishonor that the three chiefs had brought to high tribal office disturbed Four Horns. He concluded the tribe must take strong measures to restore respect and integrity to the chieftaincy. He decided to abdicate, skip over his own sons, and turn to his nephew, Sitting Bull, for the answer.

Four Horns proposed a radical idea: create a single, central leader; not just of his Hunkpapa band, but of the entire Lakota Nation. The alliance would include the Minneconjou, Oglala, Sans Arc, the Shihasapa, Two Kettles, Brule, a few Yanktonai (a Nakota dialect), and the Northern Cheyennes. The resulting coalition would be a sizable force, all under the dynamic influence of one leader: Sitting Bull.

Although it was to be more a loose consolidation of Lakota people under Hunkpapa leadership than a strongly cohesive, highly organized alliance, the union was unprecedented. As a rule, Indian clans, bands, and tribes were too independent and autonomous to be constrained by any intertribal authority, much less by one man. In this case, their acceptance of Four Horns's proposal was a well-considered break with tradition.

It was also a reflection of Sitting Bull's merit and charisma, for Sitting Bull was not the only capable leader who wanted to guide his people. Spotted Tail, chief of the Brule in the southern reaches of Lakota country, was deferring to the great white Grandfather in Washington in hopes that the president would arrange his ascent to the peak of intertribal politics. Hunkpapa tribesman Gall, who co-founded the Midnight Strong Heart Society with Sitting Bull and Crow King and was a popular leader and treaty signer, did not have the overwhelming support required. Red Cloud, a battle-tested Southern Oglala chief, leveraged his victories to secure compromises with whites but was too flexible and accommodating for the tribes. Although Crazy Horse, another Oglala standout, was arguably one of the greatest Lakota warriors ever to ride into battle, he was too solitary, reticent, and capricious to lead a multi-tribe union. In fact, Crazy Horse threw his support (and his people) behind Sitting Bull and became his staunchest ally.

Wooden Leg, one of many Northern Cheyennes who supported Sitting Bull, interpreted the intertribal dynamics and politics: "The chiefs of the different tribes met together as equals. There was only one who was considered as being above all the others. This was Sitting Bull. He was recognized as the one old man chief of all the camps combined."

In the end, Sitting Bull was the only man who optimally personified the four Lakota cardinal virtues of bravery, fortitude, generosity, and wisdom and the only one so many different tribes respected. He was experienced and successful in the hunt, in war, in politics, in spirituality, and consistent in his opposition to ceding land to European-Americans. Thus, in 1868, the Lakota chose 38-year-old Sitting Bull to lead their coalition.

The celebration of Sitting Bull's selection was as unique as it was unifying. Never before had there been such an intertribal political organization. "For your bravery on the battlefield and your reputation as the bravest warrior in all our bands," Four Horns proclaimed, "we have elected you as our war chief, leader of the entire Sioux nation. When you tell us to fight, we will fight and when you tell us to make peace, we shall make peace."

Sitting Bull was presented with a finely carved pipe depicting a seated buffalo bull, and prayers ascended heavenward to *Wakan Tanka* on the smoke that rose from the bowl. The council also gave him a beautiful war bonnet that featured ermine streamers, colorful beadwork, and immature golden eagle feathers. Finally, he was placed on his last gift, a pure white stallion, for a parade through the camps.

WHITES WERE STREAMING
WESTWARD IN WAGON TRAINS,
PASSING THROUGH, AND,
SUBSEQUENTLY, DISRUPTING

War on the PLAINS

Increasing contact between the first Americans and European-Americans, frequently escalating into conflict, soon dwarfed the feuds between tribes. Unlike other Indians, the new Caucasian arrivals were a threat to Lakota existence and culture, permanent trespassers who transformed the land and the life it supported. On the other hand, migrating European-Americans perceived the Plains Indian in a similar light. They were a dangerous anachronism, an impediment to a new life.

Whites were streaming westward in wagon trains, passing through, and, subsequently, disrupting Indian hunting grounds. The Central Pacific Railroad was building its tracks across the Central Plains, dissecting Lakota territory and disturbing the wildlife they depended on. Later, miners swarmed the Black Hills, economically and spiritually important to the Lakota. The Lakota response was to raid the European-Americans just as they raided other tribes with whom they competed for sometimes scarce resources.

To the U.S. government in the nineteenth century, the incursions into Lakota territory were natural and healthy signs of progress, and progress required a controlled, protected environment in which to

thrive. So they sent the U.S. Army to build nearly twenty forts throughout the West. Fort Lincoln, Fort Dilts, Fort Rice, Fort Yates, Fort Buford, and Fort Randall were among those that played prominently in Sitting Bull's life. However, placing soldiers in a land the Indians considered theirs further eroded their ability to live as they traditionally had. As the Lakota resisted impositions on their territory, the "long knives" (as the Lakota called the soldiers) resorted to attacks on their villages, sometimes destroying food supplies and killing people.

After the eastern Santees (four Dakota tribes) committed the Minnesota Massacre against whites in 1862, killing 400 to 800 European-Americans in an area most had thought of as peaceful farmland, the army intensified activity against all thirteen Lakota, Nakota, and Dakota tribes in their villages and hunting grounds across the northern plains. The individual Indian bands did not regard themselves as part of an organized force waging war across a broad front. However, the army, which at the time was involved in a war with the South, tended to see them that way and act accordingly. In the Battle of Killdeer Mountain of 1864 (in North Dakota), Gen. Alfred Sully and his army killed more than 100 plains Indians who had never been within 750 miles of the Minnesota Massacre.

Irate Indians, including those led by Sitting Bull, participated in many raids, burning supplies and other property. And soldiers followed them wherever they went. Sitting Bull's people headed further north and west to avoid conflict. But in late 1864, trauma pierced Sitting Bull's heart and finally turned him irreversibly against the white man.

On November 29, Col. J. M. Chivington, with about 700 Third Colorado Volunteer soldiers, attacked Black Kettle's friendly band of Southern Cheyennes on Sand Creek in what is now Colorado and killed more than 100 people, two-thirds of whom were women and children. Outrage was widespread and retaliation swift. Indians, who on their part did not always distinguish between the various groups of European-Americans—soldiers, militia, or armed settlers—

16

murdered travelers and plundered their wagon trains. The U.S. Army responded in kind with a fresh round of assaults against the Lakota.

Through the distractions of war, Sitting Bull still yearned for calm and harmony. He knew peace was possible, if only the white man would stand by the promises made in treaties. The requests were nothing new: (1) close the trails and shut off incoming traffic; (2) dismantle the forts; (3) halt the steamboats and miners; (4) banish all non-Indians (except traders). Sitting Bull wanted the people to live the free life of the Plains Indian culture and not the limited reservation life. He felt the treaty measures were necessary to prevent the whites from destroying Lakota country, eliminating the buffalo, and starving his people. If the government would honor the treaty guarantees that it had pledged earlier, peace would prevail. If not, he would make war.

"I have a message for the Grandfather [President Grant]," Sitting Bull pleaded. "I do not want anyone to bother my people. I want them to live in peace. I myself have plans for my people, and if they follow my plans, they will never want. They will never hunger. I wish for traders only, and no soldiers on my reservation. *Wakan Tanka* gave us this land, and we are at home here. I will not have my people robbed. We can live if we can keep our Black Hills. We do not want to eat from the Grandfather's hand. We can feed ourselves."

The Fort Laramie Treaty of 1868 was an attempt at compromise. It created the Great Sioux Reservation and directed all Lakota to live there. They could still pursue a buffalo-hunting economy but were strongly encouraged to pursue farming instead. On reservation settlements, they would receive rations of clothing and food but have to heed the rules of the white agent in charge and send their children to reservation schools.

The contest over the Black Hills stands out as an example of the lack of cultural empathy between the two peoples. The *Paha Sapa* ("Hills that are Black") were a sacred wellspring of Indian strength, survival, and spirituality. They were also a treasure of gold to prospectors. Treaty reserved the Black Hills for the use of the Lakota.

Only the military and other government employees were allowed to be there. However, in spite of this ban, fifteen thousand miners had rushed into the hills.

The government didn't feel it could control the incursion of European-Americans using the same methods it used against the Lakota and chose instead to invoke its right to develop the Black Hills. This right was in the treaties but perhaps not fully understood by the nomadic bands. Sitting Bull and other hunting-band leaders did not want to sell *Paha Sapa* because it was a special reserve of wild game and plant life that the Lakota could always go to when scarcity of buffalo threatened their existence.

While government discussions focused on paying the Lakotas for how much gold might be extracted from the Black Hills, Sitting Bull's concerns were based on their irreplaceable value as a sacred preserve and their critical importance to his people as a "Food Pack."

Although Sitting Bull and other hunting-band leaders had never agreed to live on reservations, the government policy throughout the West had been to contain and settle the indigenous people so settlers could develop the land in conformance with a European-style economy.

So, in December 1875, the U.S. Indian Commissioner called Sitting Bull's band "untamable and hostile." The authorities issued an ultimatum for the Lakota to report to a reservation agency immediately if they wanted to avoid an army roundup. The ultimatum gave the Indians until January 31, 1876 to obey, but the agencies were not notified until the early winter of 1875. At the time, the Lakota were 250 miles away from the agencies at their snow-covered winter camp on the Powder River, totally unaware of the ultimatum and its consequences.

When no "renegade" Lakotas reported to any of the respective agencies by February 1, 1876, the War Department ordered the army to bring them in. After his initial expedition failed to make progress in the deep snow and sub-zero temperatures, Gen. George "Three Stars" Crook made good on his orders in March. His troops attacked the Cheyenne and Oglala village of Two Moons and He Dog on the Powder River, burning all of the provisions and tipis as they went.

18

They also took half of the Indian horses—but only temporarily. The next night warriors took the ponies back. Some who escaped the raid rode 60 miles in blizzard conditions before locating a big Lakota camp. Sitting Bull took them in, fed, clothed, and outfitted them and then asked his own people to double up in their tipis so they would have lodging.

Later, on the banks of the Tongue River, Tatanka-Iyotanka delivered a stirring speech to the tribal leaders staying in his encampment—Hunkpapa, Santee, Yanktonai, Oglala, Minneconjou, Sans Arc, Brule, Two Kettles, Cheyenne, and a few Arapaho.

> Hear me, friends. We have now to deal with another people, small and feeble when our forefathers first met them, but now great and overbearing. This nation is like a spring freshet; it overruns its banks and destroys all who are in its path. We cannot dwell side by side. Only seven years ago we made a treaty by which we were assured that the buffalo country would remain ours forever. Now they threaten to take that from us also. My brothers, shall we submit? Or shall we say to them: "First kill me before you can take possession of my fatherland?"

Sitting Bull fanned the fire that he knew burned in all of them when he said, "We are an island of Indians in a lake of whites. We must stand together or they will rub us out separately. These soldiers have come shooting; they want war. All right, we'll give it to them."

A Vision of VICTORY

Tatanka-Iyotanka decided it was time to commune with the Almighty. With sweet sage on his pipe and holy tobacco burning in the bowl, he prayed to Wakan Tanka, "My God, save me and give me all my wild game animals. Bring them near me so that my people may have plenty to eat this winter. Let good men on earth have more power, so that all nations may be strong and successful. Let them be of good heart, so that all Lakota people may get along well and be happy. If you do this for me, I will perform the Sun-Gazing Dance and give you a whole buffalo."

On June 4 through 7, 1876, he fulfilled this vow. In the Rosebud Creek Valley, what became known as "Sitting Bull's Sun Dance" was held beneath the shadow of Deer Medicine Rocks. Black Moon was the sun dance chief and Sitting Bull, head dancer. Jumping Bull came

CEREMONIAL TOBACCO OFFERINGS

to the center of the medicine lodge with a sharp awl and knife blade. Sitting Bull sat against the sacred center pole as his adopted brother began cutting pieces of skin from Sitting Bull's forearms, fifty chunks from each. Soon, his arms were totally covered with blood as he gave himself to the Almighty. Painful as it must have been, Sitting Bull sat quietly while the Assiniboine sliced his flesh.

After the blood offering was complete, Sitting Bull stood up, faced the sun and center pole, and began to dance. He bobbed up and down, gazing at the sun and pulsating to the beat of the drum. Constantly dancing, shuffling to and fro, the blood finally clotting in his wounds, but not before the scarlet blanket pleased the Great Mysterious One. He danced all day, that night, and into the next day. No food. No water. No stopping. The next afternoon, he began swerving, then faltering, indicating he was going into a medicine trance, the unconscious pool from which sacred visions flow.

Several of those present grabbed Sitting Bull and gently laid him down before he could fall and hurt himself. For several suspenseful minutes, his body was motionless as he was in direct communication with *Wakan Tanka*. When he awoke, he whispered to Black Moon. It was obvious that God had received Sitting Bull's offering and prayers and, in return, had given the chief a powerful vision that foretold the future. The shaman announced, "Sitting Bull wishes to tell you about the voice he

LAKOTA-STYLE SUN DANCE STICK

just heard, which said, '*I give you these because they have no ears.*' He looked up and soldiers and some Indians on horseback were coming down like grasshoppers, with their heads down and their hats falling off. They were falling right into our camp."

The Lakota had great joy for they knew what his vision portrayed. The whites who had no ears would not listen to Sitting Bull and the other chiefs. The bluecoats who fell into their camp upside down were their defeated enemies. *Wakan Tanka* was taking care of *His* people.

Sitting Bull quickly warned his people not to take the spoils of war: no guns, no clothes, no horses. Destroy the soldiers but leave their goods alone. The chieftain told them that if they took the whites' possessions, their tribe would be cursed.

Everyone believed Tatanka-Iyotanka's vision because his prophecies had come true so many times before. Even the Ree (Arikara) scouts who discovered remnants of the huge Lakota camp and Sitting Bull's sun dance medicine lodge (on June 24) warned Lt. Col. George Armstrong Custer that the Lakota were assured of victory. It was clear to the scouts that the camp was large and the people full of confidence.

Shortly after the sun dance, needing to search elsewhere for game and forage, Sitting Bull and his council decided to move their camp west to Greasy Grass (the Little Bighorn) River. He had his hands full trying to keep all those tribes together and so many people fed.

Custer and his Seventh Cavalry were part of Gen. Alfred Terry's thousand-man force that was moving westward from Fort Abraham Lincoln to find Sitting Bull's encampment. On June 25 they approached the Little Bighorn camp. Custer sent Maj. Marcus Reno and a battalion of 175 soldiers, Indian scouts, and attached personnel to attack from the south while Custer and another 210 men skirted east of the camp along a ridgeline. Capt. Frederick Benteen brought up the rear with the mule pack train and more troopers.

The first dwellings Major Reno's forces encountered were Sitting Bull's Hunkpapa circle of tipis. When Reno's force charged from the south, around 2:45 p.m., "the very earth seemed to grow

THE
LIFE
AND
TIMES
of
SITTING
BULL

1831
Born near the Grand River in the northern Great Plains

1845
Strikes first coup in battle and receives his adult name, Sitting Bull

1860s
Violence between settlers, soldiers, and Lakota intensifies. Eight Lakota tribes form a coalition and look to Sitting Bull as a leader.

1868
Fort Laramie Treaty creates the Great Sioux Reservation and directs all Lakota to live there.

DECEMBER 6
1875
U.S. Indian Commissioner declares Sitting Bull's band "untamable" and orders them to report to a reservation by January 31, 1876.

MARCH
1876
General George Crook sets out to find free-roaming Lakota band and bring them to the reservation.

JUNE 4–7
1876
Sitting Bull's
Sun Dance

JUNE 25–26
1876
The Battle
of the Little
Bighorn

JULY 20
1881
Surrenders
at Fort
Buford,
North
Dakota.

1885
Travels with
Buffalo Bill
Cody's "Wild
West Show."

1888
The Sioux Act
reduces the
Great Sioux
Reservation
by more than
nine million
acres.

DEC. 15
1890
Sitting Bull
shot to death
at Standing
Rock
Reservation.

Indians," Reno reported. Within thirty minutes, over a quarter of the soldiers had been killed. Sitting Bull later said he wanted the rest of Reno's troops to leave so they would tell what happened.

At forty-five years of age, Sitting Bull was old enough to defend his family, the women, children, and his village but not young enough to participate in the attacks, gun battles, or coup counting. So, Sitting Bull gave One Bull, his nephew and adopted son, his treasured shield and urged him to "Brave up."

Indians from the Cheyenne, Brule, and Oglala circles spotted Custer's five companies topping the bluffs and then descending Medicine Tail Coulee, toward the Little Bighorn River. They knew the troops were putting themselves in a position to cut off the villagers trying to escape to the north. Fresh warriors crossed the Little Bighorn and swiftly rode to meet the threat. Hunkpapa and Minneconjou, freed up by Reno's retreat, also joined the fray. Custer's

LT. COL. GEORGE ARMSTRONG
CUSTER IN 1872

battalion, which had split into two wings, withdrew to Battle Ridge. With no cover nearby, the long knives dismounted and fired at the charging warriors. The five companies soon began to disintegrate, with survivors retreating to an area that would later be dubbed Last Stand Hill. The hill was quickly engulfed in such a cloud of dust and gunsmoke that one could only guess what the carnage of man and horse was like. Lieutenant Colonel Custer had fought his last battle. He was found with a bullet in his left temple and one in the chest. Everyone in his battalion was dead.

Tatanka-Iyotanka's prophecy had come true with a vengeance. Never before had Indians managed such a complete victory over the U.S. Army. Unfortunately, Sitting Bull's people could not resist the saddles, provisions, guns, and ammunition. Looting was widespread and the victory was short-lived. The Battle of the Little Bighorn actually marked the beginning of a steady descent to the end for the off-reservation Lakota and Sitting Bull.

Many times, Sitting Bull was asked about the Battle of the Little Bighorn. Many times, he replied, "I feel sorry that too many were killed on each side but when Indians must fight, they must. I had to fight because I was attacked. Even a bird will protect its nest. Perhaps the whites think they can exterminate us but God will not permit it."

After the battle, the combined village broke up into smaller groupings and scattered. As much as anything, the search for buffalo determined the direction and deployment of tribes. The chiefs decided that it would be advantageous to subdivide back down to customary tribal levels or even smaller units, primarily for hunting purposes. Feeding thousands camped together proved too great a challenge.

Little did the Indians know how stunned the nation was by the defeat of Custer and his troops. Though people knew there was resistance by the native population, the deaths of 263 men and their charismatic leader caused a public cry for retaliation. President Grant and Congress were ready to give the army all of the men, money, and materiel they needed to quell Lakota troubles for good. New forts would go up in buffalo country as soon as weather permitted.

27

INTERLUDE

Immediately after the historic battle, many Oglalas, Minneconjous, Sans Arc, and Hunkpapas were still together. Some of these were on their way to agencies to surrender when they were intercepted by General Crook, who recovered some items from the Battle of the Little Bighorn. Crazy Horse and the Oglalas turned south. The other three tribes stayed together until Col. "Bear Coat" Miles pressured several Minneconjou and Sans Arc chiefs to surrender. During the "winter of despair" (1876–1877), bands of Lakota and Cheyenne not only had to deal with the normal hazards of winter but also with intensified attacks by soldiers. The alternative was unconditional surrender. Neither choice fulfilled life while either could mean death.

When most of the other bands had splintered off, Sitting Bull headed north of the border into Canada in May 1877 with 400 exhausted and starving Hunkpapas and 135 tattered Lakota lodges to find peace. He prayed that his dealings with "Grandmother" Queen Victoria would be more favorable than those with the Grandfather to the south.

While staying at Pinto Horse Butte near Wood Mountain, Saskatchewan, the chief tried to secure some land that would be set

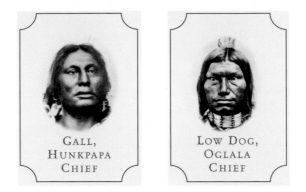

GALL,
HUNKPAPA
CHIEF

LOW DOG,
OGLALA
CHIEF

up as an Indian reserve. His requests were denied. However, he and his people were free to hunt buffalo from the plentiful herds in the area. He was welcome in Canada as long as he obeyed the laws and did not make raids on whites or soldiers south of the border. Sitting Bull continued to lose followers.

Concurrently, on May 6, 1877, Crazy Horse and 889 Oglalas gave up at Camp Robinson, Nebraska. Crazy Horse had decided there was nothing for him in Canada. His relative, Brule chief Spotted Tail, had talked him into giving up even though he believed that to do so might prove fatal. When Crazy Horse turned himself in, he did not anticipate becoming a prisoner. In September, when an army post commandant tried to jail him, the war chief resisted. While jailers (and his friend Little Bigman) tried restraining him, a soldier stabbed Crazy Horse with a bayonet. A few hours later, the famous warrior lay dead.

News of his comrade's death hit Sitting Bull hard. Tatanka-Iyotanka's attempts to defend the Lakota homeland from white encroachment and to protect his people from military assaults had failed and his following was shrinking. But he was still the Indian who had defeated Custer, the last chieftain who had not surrendered to the U. S. Army, and the only Lakota leader to believe that native life could still be sustained by the buffalo.

When Sitting Bull led his followers into Canada in 1877, the plains between Wood Mountain and Cypress Hills were filled with bounteous herds of buffalo. The northern immigration of Lakotas continued after the government closed the Red Cloud and Spotted Tail Agencies. As Canada kept her doors open to natives, more than a thousand Oglalas took refuge there. By the time White Bird arrived with enough Nez Perce to fill four dozen tipis, the stock of buffalo meat proved to be not only finite but also dwindling.

The Canadian tribes—Blood, Blackfeet, Piegan, Cree, Salteaux, Sarsi, and Slotas (Metis)—blamed the newcomers for depleting the herds of bison on which their survival and culture also depended. Hide hunters were racing the Indians to the buffalo and buffalo habitat was contracting as stockmen fenced off rangeland for their steers and sheep. By 1881, the vast herds of buffalo were dangerously small, by some counts on the brink of extinction.

Sitting Bull had fewer than 200 followers left in Canada. Most were old relatives who missed their homeland and a good meal. Hunting was bad on both sides of the border. The chief's repeated appeals to the Canadian government for food rations were often denied. Canadian officials had begun to see Sitting Bull as a liability and wanted him to return to the States and surrender. Three major defections—by Gall, Crow King, Low Dog, and their respective followers, severely eroded Bull's base of support and intensified the hunger and homesickness in those who were left.

The chief decided to end his four-year stay in Canada and return to his homeland because he could not bear to see his people starving. He was often warned that he might be given the same reception as Crazy Horse. However, his pride, leadership, heart, and independence finally had to succumb to defeat—and to white control.

A time to SURRENDER

Tatanka-Iyotanka was advised to report to Fort Buford, in North Dakota. He was to give up his guns and ponies and, in exchange, would receive a "full pardon" for his past. He was promised he would be sent to the Standing Rock Agency at Fort Yates where other Hunkpapas were being held. Sitting Bull arrived at Fort Buford with forty-three families on July 19, 1881. The next day he handed his Winchester rifle to Crow Foot, his eight-year-old son, and indicated that he was the last Lakota chief to surrender his gun. Crow Foot passed it on to Fort Buford's commander, Maj. David Brotherton. The chieftain did not want to capitulate directly and chose to soften the blow with the insulation of another generation.

As he had done at so many other critical junctures in his life, he composed a song:

"A warrior I have been,
Now it's all over.
A hard time I have."

With his small band of extended family, Sitting Bull boarded a steamboat for the three-day float down the Missouri River to Standing Rock Agency and to a world transformed beyond their wildest dreams. The last of the free Hunkpapas got off at Fort Yates

CROW FOOT, SITTING BULL'S SON, WHO
HELPED THE GREAT LEADER SURRENDER
AT FORT BUFORD

but the chief was not among them. The generals had second thoughts about re-uniting the tribe and its great leader. They aborted the reunion and, instead, decided to ship Tatanka-Iyotanka further downstream to Fort Randall.

Sitting Bull suffered the most miserable and most boring span of his life while he was exiled for two years at Fort Randall. Long gone and far removed were the old traditional days of constant motion: following the buffalo, counting coups, being chased, waging war, dodging death. Now he sat still day in, day out, with no end in sight.

When he was finally released to Standing Rock Reservation, Sitting Bull assumed that he would resume his roles as head chief and medicine man of the Hunkpapa and pre-eminent chief of all Lakotas. Unfortunately, the powerful agent on Standing Rock did not see it that way.

James McLaughlin was a strict, seasoned agent whose goal was to transform the Lakota into law-abiding farmers. He hoped to acculturate the Indians through agriculture, schools, church missions, and the judicial system. To that end, he controlled rations, the Indian police, and Indian courts.

For all that Sitting Bull had been through, he still held strongly to his cultural beliefs and traditional practices. He retained the respect of his people and his will to lead. However, McLaughlin did not want to encourage, support, or help Sitting Bull in retaining his chieftainship or return to any influential position. The agent viewed the old man as a stubborn obstructionist and power-seeking, rabble-rousing troublemaker. Each saw the other as a barrier to his personal goals and professional ambitions, McLaughlin and Tatanka-Iyotanka despised each other from their first encounter.

Wanting to get off the reservation and away from McLaughlin's tight grasp, the chief consented to be in a traveling exhibition tour. He was also curious about the new, white world outside Fort Yates. Hence, in 1884, Sitting Bull was publicized as "The Great Slayer of General Custer" and began a tour around the United States. As the Hunkpapas acted out some traditions on stage and discussed their culture in the Lakota dialect, a white person told the audience

SITTING BULL &
BUFFALO BILL CODY

about the Battle of the Little Bighorn and how Sitting Bull had killed Long Hair Custer.

In 1885, Buffalo Bill Cody stole Sitting Bull away from the theater pageant and put the chief on horseback in his traveling "Wild West Show." Sitting Bull made $50 per week (with a bonus of $125 when he first signed up) and much more selling his photos and autographs. Still espousing the Hunkpapa virtue of generosity, he gave most of his money away to beggars and shoe shiners on the streets. He got along well with Buffalo Bill and especially enjoyed watching the accurate shooting of Annie Oakley, whom he dubbed "Little Sure Shot." Cody wanted to take Sitting Bull with the show to England but the sashwearer turned him down. When the two participated in their last performance together, Buffalo Bill gave Sitting Bull the beautiful, gray roan horse that he had ridden in the shows.

REDUCTION

In 1887 Congress introduced the General Allotment Act. It stipulated that reservation land would be removed from tribal ownership and then allotted, in 160-acre parcels, to each family head. After the lots were doled out to all who applied and qualified, the government could buy the remaining land and open it up to settlement. Original offers put the value of land at fifty cents per acre.

The next year, the Sioux Act subdivided the Great Sioux Reservation into six smaller reserves: Standing Rock, Cheyenne River, Crow Creek, Rosebud, Pine Ridge, and Lower Brule. Each would include the acreage necessary for all tribal allotments. After all allocations were distributed and reservation boundaries redrawn, the government had reduced the Great Sioux Reservation by between nine and ten million acres.

Sitting Bull had never been willing to relinquish one square foot of Lakota land and was not about to start now. He warned other reservation chiefs that the government offer was just a ploy to further reduce the land under Indian control. Even the price was totally inadequate, especially when the government proposed to turn around and sell the land for $1.25 an acre to white homesteaders.

At first, Sitting Bull managed to keep Charging Bear (John Grass), Gall, Mad Bear, and Big Head united in their opposition to ratify either of the land-reducing acts. The negotiations between the government's commissioners and tribal officials dragged on for months, then almost a year, in Lakota Country and back in the nation's capital. Rumors and counter-rumors ran rampant, one speculating that if the Indians did not sign, the government would reduce their rations. After much lobbying by agent McLaughlin and General Crook, among others, the acts were ratified, and Lakota land was halved.

When the whites won again, many Indians were left agitated if not angry, bewildered if not bitter. And instead of realizing what had just happened, Lakota turned against each other. Sitting Bull was left with the depressing realization that life on a now-smaller reservation would never be as good as it once was out on the open prairie, heading into the wind on a lightning-fast pony, running down buffalo, and dancing at the evening feast thereafter.

Again, a groundswell of gossip began to circulate concerning the government cutting food rations to the Indians once they took possession of the excluded real estate. Assurances from the commission did not allay the Lakota's apprehension. And in fact, scarcely two weeks after the acts were approved, reservation agents were notified that their meat allocations had been reduced by several million pounds.

The Ghost Dance THREAT

Everyone was missing the glory days of yesteryear, yearning for salvation, when a curious voice of hope called out to the Indian people. Kicking Bear, a Minneconjou mystic from the Cheyenne River Agency, introduced Sitting Bull in 1890 to the teachings of Wovoka, a Paiute holy man, who offered a promising future to all Indians. He had experienced a great vision during a solar eclipse and was temporarily taken to heaven where he was shown "the way."

Wovoka declared that the new faith admonished believers to be peaceful, honest, pure, and loving. The movement featured basic tenets and practices of Indian spirituality blended with the teachings of Christianity. Salvation focused on performing a sacred ghost dance where the believers encountered and communed with their deceased relatives. The faithful would ultimately live in a utopian paradise where the Indian Christ would call the dead to life, where whites would be absent, and the buffalo would once again cover the prairie. Believers would live eternally in a land where all Indians of the past would unite with those of the present. There would be no sickness, despair, or unhappiness, and all tribes would live in harmony.

Since Kicking Bear initially went to Sitting Bull, agent McLaughlin mistook the chief for the high priest and instigator of

the ghost dance religion on Standing Rock. At first, Sitting Bull did not accept all the tenets of the new faith. In due time, though, he erected a tipi near the ghost grounds and helped the dancers interpret their visions. Eventually, he entered the circle, took part in a few summer ceremonies of 1890, and, based on his belief in religious freedom, became a defender of Wovoka's teachings on the reservation though he did not direct the dances.

As one of the most reputable holy men of his time, Tatanka-Iyotanka's participation in the ghost dance lent the movement credibility and reinforced its appeal. In fact, the dance circle and worship services were held at an open area near his residence on the banks of the Grand River.

Increased publicity about the religion led to concern among whites. Apprehensive about physical reprisals by the public, police, and military, the ghost dancers declared that their creamy muslin ghost shirts gave them courage and protection because they were bullet-proof (a Kicking Bear addendum to Wovoka's original ghost dance interpretation). This further inflamed whites, who then assumed that Indians were planning an armed confrontation. Agent McLaughlin, who saw outside animosity build against the ghost dance movement, grew concerned about the public perception of his ability to control the Indians.

Sitting Bull felt, and said, that his religious beliefs were nobody else's business. He affirmed that the ghost dance did not endanger anyone and those who participated meant no harm to anyone. Citing scores of different denominations and religions of the non-Indian, he rightfully noted that whites worshiped the way they wanted with no external interference so Indians should have the same right.

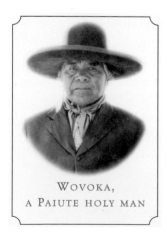

WOVOKA,
A PAIUTE HOLY MAN

As emotions and politics surrounding the ghost dance continued
to heat up by the day on all Lakota reservations, agitation replaced
reason and hysteria erased understanding. Nearby communities
feared an armed Indian insurrection and asked for protection from
the ghost dance worshippers. The Department of the Interior called
in the army, but Indian administrators, like McLaughlin, who did not
want to be supplanted by external control, tried to come up with a
way to handle the situation on their own.

The Death of
SITTING
BULL

Grave monument in
Mobridge, South
Dakota

Sitting Bull planned to travel south to the Pine Ridge
Reservation soon and McLaughlin suspected it was to share a
ghost dance with his kin or plot some kind of revolt. Either
way, the agent decided the only way to control Sitting Bull
was to arrest him.

One day in November 1890, Sitting Bull was out
in the rough country looking for the old gray roan that
Buffalo Bill had given him. He was very much alone,
about three miles out, except for the animal and bird
people. He faintly heard a voice as he saw a meadowlark
land on a juniper branch nearby. A new song rolled out
of its beak: "Lakota will kill you." Though grieved, the
chief did not question the harsh meaning because the
bird had obviously been sent by the Great Mysterious
One. He tried forgetting the words but they continued
to echo in his mind: "Lakota will kill you."

McLaughlin, who knew the depth of Sitting Bull's
support and anticipated his resistance, had been
increasing his police force for several weeks. These
were called the *akicita*—or "Metal Breasts," and

were hired from the Indians who lived on the reservation. Finally he put out the arrest order for Tatanka-Iyotanka, using his involvement in the ghost dance as the reason. Half of his police force, including the police captain, turned in their badges and guns to protest. One Bull, as Sitting Bull's close relative, was dismissed with them. A lieutenant, Bullhead, chose his own deputies, most of whom were Yanktonai and Sihasapa Lakota (he could not get any Hunkpapa to go because many were the chief's relatives). The *akicita* were promised promotions and raises if the plan backfired and any were injured. Their families would be able to draw on increased pensions if any of them was killed. McLaughlin made sure that the Metal Breasts had a wagon "to bring Bull in" and added an ominous order: "You must not let him escape under any circumstances."

On December 15, 1890, after traveling on horseback for most of the night, the forty-four *akicita* arrived at Sitting Bull's camp on the Grand River. The predawn peace was punctuated by the sounds of owls hooting and coyotes harmonizing. The riders dismounted and took up their positions surrounding the living quarters. Flanked by Shave Head and Sgt. Red Tomahawk, Lt. Bullhead forced his way into the two-room cabin, grabbed the sleeping chief, and yanked him to his feet. The drowsy old man, who was naked and cold, requested some clothes.

The screams of Sitting Bull's wives and children awoke the sleeping settlement. Some of Tatanka-Iyotanka's faction had come from nearby homes and were shaking their fists while arguing with the police. Catch-the-Bear, one of Sitting Bull's body guards, spotted his old enemy, Bullhead, who was manhandling the chief, and warned, "You shall not take him!"

Sitting Bull avowed, "You are all Indians and the blood that runs in your veins is the same as mine. . . . You are my own people who have come as agents of the government to arrest me and stand ready to shoot down your own flesh and blood. You are cowards to come to my house in the nighttime. You are dogs to raise your hands against your own people, and you do not deserve to be called Lakota—or to live. I'm not going! Come on! Take action!"

With that resistive declaration, hot tempers replaced cold words; panic, then pandemonium, followed quickly. Catch-the-Bear raised his rifle and fired it at Bullhead's torso. As he was falling, Bullhead shot Sitting Bull through the chest. Red Tomahawk, from behind, fired another bullet into Tatanka-Iyotanka's head at point-blank range. Then Strikes-the-Kettle shot, sending a bullet into Shave Head's stomach. Before it was over, fourteen men from both camps lay dead. Lone Man, who shot and killed Catch-the-Bear, found young Crow Foot cowering under a bed after the shootout and proceeded to pistol-whip him before using his body for target practice.

The shooting acted as a Pavlovian bell to the old gray horse, which thought it was time to perform again in "The Wild West Show." He started his routine of tricks by rearing back on his rear legs with his front feet flailing in circles. The *akicita* feared that it was Sitting Bull's spirit that had entered the roan, prompting it to box in disapproval.

While much dignity and sorrow was afforded the fallen police-men, Sitting Bull was given an indigent burial at the post cemetery of Fort Yates. With no family or friends in attendance, soldier-prisoners from the guardhouse were recruited to bury the chief's wooden casket to the muted call of a lone meadowlark. James Walsh, the friendly Canadian North-West Mounted Police Commander who was the only white man that Sitting Bull ever really trusted, penned a eulogy that no one read . . . or heard:

> I am glad to learn that Sitting Bull is relieved of his miseries even if it took a bullet to do it. A man who wields such power as Sitting Bull once did, that of a King, over a wild-spirited people cannot endure abject poverty, slavery, and beggary without suffering great mental pain, and death is a relief. . . . Sitting Bull's confidence and belief in the Great Spirit was stronger than I ever saw in any other man. He trusted to him implicitly. . . . History does not tell us that a greater Indian than Bull ever lived, he was the Mohommat of his people the law and king maker of the Sioux.

Wounded KNEE

Sitting Bull's death exacerbated already heightened tensions in Indian country. Kicking Bear's interpretations of Wovoka's peaceful teachings took on a belligerent tone. Talk of bulletproof ghost shirts and whites being destroyed by cataclysmic burial seemed to imply, if not actually incite, an uprising. However, in a defensive posture, Lakota, including Sitting Bull before his death, stated they would not tolerate any interference by Caucasians who were bent on suppressing the ghost dance by force. In fact, whites could count on violent resistance by the Indians, meeting force with force, fighting fire with fire.

In turn, whites started frantic rumors that escalated the paranoia. One unfounded report indicated the Lakota were going on the warpath, attacking villages and farms, slaughtering every form of life in their path. The press printed this and other provocative articles about the Indians, whipping up a frenzy that was founded on fiction and served to help events spiral further out of control. European-Americans called for preemptive military strikes against the natives.

Two weeks after the chief's death, ghost dancers from Cheyenne River headed to the Badlands where other dancers were already holed up. They suspected that they might be rounded up and arrested, punished, or otherwise harassed. Ironically, a unit from Custer's old

Seventh Cavalry were the troops directed to move in on their location at
Wounded Knee Creek. The soldiers, who well remembered the Seventh's
defeat at the Battle of the Little Bighorn, surrounded the worshippers and
trained their Hotchkiss (rapid-firing) guns on Big Foot (Spotted Elk) and
his followers. One shot rang out, igniting the explosion. Instantly, a
thousand shots peppered the circle and initiated the terrified screams,
haphazard running, and mournful cries of the targeted victims. When the
last shot silenced the last voice, more than 150 Lakota men, women, and
children had been killed on the snow-covered creek bottom of Wounded
Knee. Twenty-eight soldiers also died in the fight.

Tatanka-Iyotanka's vision, prophecy, and warning—"Do not touch the
spoils or lust after the white man's goods lest it prove to be a curse to this
nation"—had now come full circle as the whites pored over the lifeless
forms that were frozen in grotesque agony, looking for souvenirs and
ghost shirts that had bullet holes through them.

Sitting Bull predicted and participated in the overwhelming victory at
the Battle of the Little Bighorn. More important, he foresaw and resisted
the destruction of the plains culture. Tatanka-Iyotanka asked, "Is it wicked
because my skin is red; because I am a Lakota; because I was born where
my fathers lived; because I would die for my people and country?"

further reading

- Carroll, John M., ed. *The Arrest and Killing of Sitting Bull.* Glendale, Calif.: Arthur H. Clark Co., 1986.
- Diedrich, Mark, ed. *Sitting Bull, the Collected Speeches.* Rochester, Minn.: Coyote Books, 1998.
- Fiske, Frank B. *Life and Death of Sitting Bull.* Fort Yates, N.D.: Pioneer-Arrow 1933.
- Hoover, Herbert T. "Sitting Bull," in *American Indian Leaders: Studies in Diversity,* ed. R. David Edmunds. Lincoln, Neb.: University of Nebraska Press, 1980.
- ————. *The Last Years of Sitting Bull.* Bismark, N.D.: State Historical Society of North Dakota, 1984.
- Utley, Robert M. *The Lance and the Shield: The Life and Times of Sitting Bull.* New York, N.Y.: Ballantine, 1993.
- Vestal, Stanley. *Sitting Bull: Champion of the Sioux.* Norman, Okla.: University of Oklahoma Press, 1932.
- ————. *Warpath, the True Story of the Fighting Sioux.* Lincoln, Neb.: University of Nebraska Press, 1934.